HOMECOMING

The Paintings of William H. Johnson

A Book of Postcards

National Museum of American Art

Smithsonian Institution

Published in cooperation with the
National Museum of American Art, Smithsonian Institution,
by Pomegranate Artbooks
Box 808022
Petaluma, CA 94975

ISBN 0-87654-809-5
Pomegranate Catalog No. A578

Pomegranate publishes several other postcard collections on many different subjects.
Please write to the publisher for more information.

Cover design by Riba Taylor
© 1991 Smithsonian Institution
Printed in Korea

The National Museum of American Art, Smithsonian Institution, is dedicated to the preservation, exhibition, and study of the visual arts in America. The museum, whose publications program also includes the scholarly journal *American Art*, has extensive research resources: the databases of the Inventories of American Painting and Sculpture, several image archives, and a variety of scholarly fellowships. For more information or a catalogue of publications, write: Office of Publications, National Museum of American Art, Smithsonian Institution, Washington, DC 20560.

By almost any standard, William H. Johnson (1901–1970) can be considered a major American artist. He produced hundreds of works in a virtuosic, eclectic career that spanned several decades as well as several continents. It was not until very recently, however, that his work began to receive the attention it deserves.

Born in South Carolina to a poor African-American family, Johnson moved to New York at age seventeen. Working a variety of jobs, he saved enough money to pay for an art education at the prestigious National Academy of Design. His mastery of the academy's rigorous standards gained him both numerous awards and the respect of his teachers and fellow students.

Johnson spent the late 1920s in France, absorbing the lessons of modernism. As a result, his work became more expressive and emotional. During this same period, he met and fell in love with Danish artist Holcha Krake, whom he married in 1930. The couple spent most of the '30s in Scandinavia, where Johnson's interest in primitivism and folk art began to have a noticeable impact on his work.

Returning with Holcha to the U.S. in 1938, Johnson immersed himself in the traditions of Afro-America, producing work characterized by its stunning, eloquent, folk art simplicity. A Greenwich Village resident, he became a familiar, if somewhat aloof, figure on the New York art scene. He was also a well-established part of the African-American artistic community at a time when most black artists were still riding the crest of the Harlem Renaissance.

Although Johnson enjoyed a certain degree of success as an artist in this country and abroad, financial security remained elusive. Following his wife's death in 1944, Johnson's physical and mental health declined dramatically. In a tragic and drawn-out conclusion to a life of immense creativity, Johnson spent his last twenty-three years in a state hospital on Long Island. By the time of his death in 1970, he had slipped into obscurity. After his death, his entire life's work was almost disposed of to save on storage fees, but it was rescued by friends at the last moment. Over a thousand paintings by Johnson are now part of the collection of the Smithsonian Institution's National Museum of American Art.

Homecoming: The Paintings of William H. Johnson
William H. Johnson (1901–1970)
Jitterbugs (I), c. 1940–41
Oil on wood, 39¾ x 31¼ in.

Pomegranate • Box 808022 • Petaluma, CA 94975

W.H.Johnson

Homecoming: The Paintings of William H. Johnson
William H. Johnson (1901–1970)
Early Morning Work, c. 1940
Oil on burlap, 38½ x 45⅜ in.

Pomegranate • Box 808022 • Petaluma, CA 94975

Homecoming: The Paintings of William H. Johnson
William H. Johnson (1901–1970)
Mom and Dad (or *Portrait of a Lady with Kittens*), 1944
Oil on paperboard, 31 x 25⅜ in.

Pomegranate • Box 808022 • Petaluma, CA 94975

Homecoming: The Paintings of William H. Johnson
William H. Johnson (1901–1970)
City Gates, Kairouan, 1932
Watercolor and pencil on paper, 19¾ x 25⅝ in.

Pomegranate • Box 808022 • Petaluma, CA 94975

Homecoming: The Paintings of William H. Johnson
William H. Johnson (1901–1970)
Nat Turner, c. 1945
Oil on paperboard, 31³/₈ x 25⁷/₈ in.

Pomegranate • Box 808022 • Petaluma, CA 94975

Homecoming: The Paintings of William H. Johnson
William H. Johnson (1901–1970)
Nude, c. 1939
Oil on burlap, 29¾ x 38¼ in.

Pomegranate • Box 808022 • Petaluma, CA 94975

National Museum of American Art
Smithsonian Institution
Gift of the Harmon Foundation, 1967.59.1135

Homecoming: The Paintings of William H. Johnson
William H. Johnson (1901–1970)
Man in a Vest, c. 1939
Oil on burlap, 30 x 24 in.

Pomegranate • Box 808022 • Petaluma, CA 94975

Homecoming: The Paintings of William H. Johnson
William H. Johnson (1901–1970)
Mount Calvary, c. 1944
Oil on paperboard, 27¾ x 33⅛ in.

Pomegranate • Box 808022 • Petaluma, CA 94975

National Museum of American Art
Smithsonian Institution
Gift of the Harmon Foundation, 1967.59.979
© Smithsonian Institution

Homecoming: The Paintings of William H. Johnson
William H. Johnson (1901–1970)
Midnight Sun, Lofoten, 1937
Oil on burlap, 41⅝ x 59⅛ in.

Pomegranate • Box 808022 • Petaluma, CA 94975

Homecoming: The Paintings of William H. Johnson
William H. Johnson (1901–1970)
Street Musicians, c. 1940
Oil on wood, 36⅜ x 28¼ in.

Pomegranate • Box 808022 • Petaluma, CA 94975

National Museum of American Art
Smithsonian Institution
Gift of the Harmon Foundation, 1967.59.670

Homecoming: The Paintings of William H. Johnson
William H. Johnson (1901–1970)
Young Pastry Cook, c. 1928–30
Oil on canvas, 31¼ x 22⅝ in.

Pomegranate • Box 808022 • Petaluma, CA 94975

National Museum of American Art
Smithsonian Institution
Gift of the Harmon Foundation, 1967.59.693
© Smithsonian Institution

Homecoming: The Paintings of William H. Johnson
William H. Johnson (1901–1970)
I Baptize Thee, c. 1940
Oil on burlap, 38$\frac{1}{4}$ x 45$\frac{1}{2}$ in.

Pomegranate • Box 808022 • Petaluma, CA 94975

Homecoming: The Paintings of William H. Johnson
William H. Johnson (1901–1970)
Willie and Holcha, c. 1935
Hand-colored woodcut, 13¾ x 17 in.

Pomegranate • Box 808022 • Petaluma, CA 94975

National Museum of American Art
Smithsonian Institution
Gift of the Harmon Foundation, 1967.59.793

Homecoming: The Paintings of William H. Johnson
William H. Johnson (1901–1970)
Cafe, c. 1939–40
Oil on fiberboard, 36½ x 28⅛ in.

Pomegranate • Box 808022 • Petaluma, CA 94975

National Museum of American Art
Smithsonian Institution
Gift of the Harmon Foundation, 1967.59.669

Homecoming: The Paintings of William H. Johnson
William H. Johnson (1901–1970)
Old Salt, Denmark, c. 1931–32
Oil on burlap, 31 x 25⅜ in.

Pomegranate • Box 808022 • Petaluma, CA 94975

National Museum of American Art
Smithsonian Institution
Gift of the Harmon Foundation, 1967.59.758
© Smithsonian Institution

W. H. Johnson

Homecoming: The Paintings of William H. Johnson

William H. Johnson (1901–1970)
Moon Over Harlem, c. 1943–44
Oil on wood, 28½ x 35¾ in.

Pomegranate • Box 808022 • Petaluma, CA 94975

Homecoming: The Paintings of William H. Johnson
William H. Johnson (1901–1970)
Self-Portrait with Pipe, c. 1937
Oil on canvas, 35 x 28 in.

Pomegranate • Box 808022 • Petaluma, CA 94975

Homecoming: The Paintings of William H. Johnson
William H. Johnson (1901–1970)
Red Cross Nurses Handing Out Wool for Knitting, c. 1942
Tempera, pen and ink on paper, 17⁷/₁₆ x 21⁷/₈ in.

Pomegranate • Box 808022 • Petaluma, CA 94975

National Museum of American Art
Smithsonian Institution
Gift of the Harmon Foundation, 1967.59.168

Homecoming: The Paintings of William H. Johnson
William H. Johnson (1901–1970)
Joe Louis and Unidentified Boxer, c. 1939–42
Tempera, pen and ink on paper, 18 x 22 in.

Pomegranate • Box 808022 • Petaluma, CA 94975

Homecoming: The Paintings of William H. Johnson
William H. Johnson (1901–1970)
Village Houses, Cagnes-sur-Mer, c. 1928–29
Oil on canvas, 31 x 25⅛ in.

Pomegranate • Box 808022 • Petaluma, CA 94975

National Museum of American Art
Smithsonian Institution
Gift of the Harmon Foundation, 1967.59.691

Homecoming: The Paintings of William H. Johnson
William H. Johnson (1901–1970)
Ten Miles to J Camp, c. 1942
Gouache, pen and ink on paper, 13¾ x 17⅞ in.

Pomegranate • Box 808022 • Petaluma, CA 94975

National Museum of American Art
Smithsonian Institution
Gift of the Harmon Foundation, 1967.59.1071

Homecoming: The Paintings of William H. Johnson
William H. Johnson (1901–1970)
Jacobia Hotel, 1930
Oil on canvas, 19⅞ x 23¾ in.

Pomegranate • Box 808022 • Petaluma, CA 94975

National Museum of American Art
Smithsonian Institution
Gift of the Harmon Foundation, 1967.59.741

Homecoming: The Paintings of William H. Johnson
William H. Johnson (1901–1970)
Chain Gang, c. 1939
Oil on wood, 45¾ x 38½ in.

Pomegranate • Box 808022 • Petaluma, CA 94975

National Museum of American Art
Smithsonian Institution
Gift of the Harmon Foundation, 1967.59.675
© Smithsonian Institution

Homecoming: The Paintings of William H. Johnson
William H. Johnson (1901–1970)
Self-Portrait, 1929
Oil on canvas, 23¼ x 18¼ in.

Pomegranate • Box 808022 • Petaluma, CA 94975

National Museum of American Art
Smithsonian Institution
Gift of the Harmon Foundation, 1967.59.762

Homecoming: The Paintings of William H. Johnson
William H. Johnson (1901–1970)
Underground Railroad, c. 1945
Oil on paperboard, 33⅜ x 36⅜ in.

Pomegranate • Box 808022 • Petaluma, CA 94975

National Museum of American Art
Smithsonian Institution
Gift of the Harmon Foundation, 1967.59.645

Homecoming: The Paintings of William H. Johnson
William H. Johnson (1901–1970)
Lamentation (or *Descent from the Cross*), c. 1944
Oil on fiberboard, 29⅛ x 33¼ in.

Pomegranate • Box 808022 • Petaluma, CA 94975

National Museum of American Art
Smithsonian Institution
Gift of the Harmon Foundation, 1967.59.981

Homecoming: The Paintings of William H. Johnson
William H. Johnson (1901–1970)
Soldiers' Morning Bath, c. 1942
Tempera, pen and ink on paper, 16 x 20⅝ in.

Pomegranate • Box 808022 • Petaluma, CA 94975

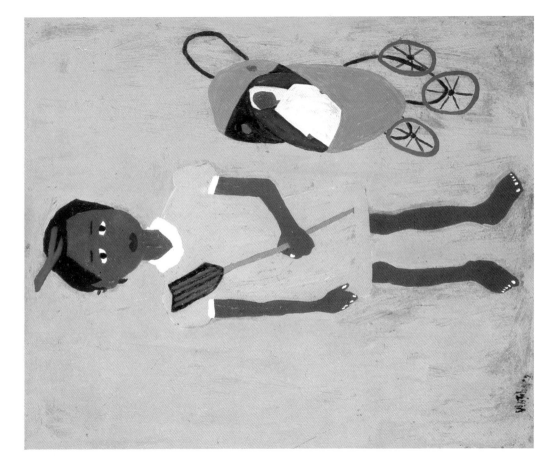

Homecoming: The Paintings of William H. Johnson
William H. Johnson (1901–1970)
L'il Sis, 1944
Oil on paperboard, 26 x 21¼ in.

Pomegranate • Box 808022 • Petaluma, CA 94975

National Museum of American Art
Smithsonian Institution
Gift of the Harmon Foundation, 1967.59.1023

Homecoming: The Paintings of William H. Johnson
William H. Johnson (1901–1970)
Self-Portrait, c. 1934–35
Oil on burlap, 26⅛ x 26⅛ in.

Pomegranate • Box 808022 • Petaluma, CA 94975

Homecoming: The Paintings of William H. Johnson
William H. Johnson (1901–1970)
Going to Church, c. 1940–41
Oil on burlap, 38⅛ x 45½ in.

Pomegranate • Box 808022 • Petaluma, CA 94975